o Be or Not To Be,
Innit.

A yoof-speak guide to Shakespeare

by Martin Baum

A Bright Pen Book

ISBN 978-0-755210-82-4

Authors OnLine Ltd
19 The Cinques
Gamlingay, Sandy
Bedfordshire SG19 3NU
England

Author's Website:-
www.baumskifilks.com

This book is also available in e-book format, details of which are available at www.authorsonline.co.uk

For Liz and Josh

Martin Baum - aka Baumski – is a member of the Writers' Guild of Great Britain but, surprisingly, is not a descendent of William Shakespeare but is an accredited satirical writer of plays and songs. He has a website: baumskifilks.com where a vast selection of Martin's parody songs can be found.

He lives on the South coast of England and believes that the carbon footprint belongs to Bigfoot.

CONTENTS

INTRODUCTION

Alas, poor Shakespeare, we knew him well but not exactly in a way we used to. If Will was with us today I think he'd feel duty bound to reflect life as it really is in the 21st century; living, as he would be, on the front line in Stratford upon Avon with his fit bitch Ann Hathaway.

However, nowadays Shakespeare isn't as cool as he used to be because a lot of people think he's boring and lacks street cred. Perhaps. But if the Bard *was* living today I reckon he'd say "Am I bovvered?" After all, for a man accredited with the greatest literature ever written, what would he have to prove?

No, if William Shakespeare was of this age I am certain that he would still be writing in the Globe turf, getting loads of respect from the Stratford upon Avon massive and producing works of pure genius like *'Romeo and His Fit Bitch Jools'*, *'De Taming of de Bitch'*, *'Macbeff'* and *'Two Geezas of Verona'*.

However, for all the purists reading this brief introduction I would just like to say that this abridged collection of some of Shakespeare's finest work has been mindful to stay true to the original format by retaining all the important sexist, duplicitous, cross-dressing and violent moments that made William Shakespeare well wicked.

Respect.

ALL'S SWEET THAT ENDS SWEET, INNIT

Helena was de orphaned bitch of de well famous quack doctor who, with de geeza called Bertram and his Countess muvva, had been living in de Rossillion turf forever.

Although they had been well full of respect for each other, over de years, Helena had been falling for Bertram big time and wanted to get all jiggy jiggy with him. Bertram, though, being de all macho geeza, didn't really care coz he fought she was well minging. But his muvva, on de other hand, quite liked de idea of Helena becoming her son's bitch.

But true lurv was dealt de cruel blow when de King of France geeza was taken all deathly ill in Froggyland and without de moment of hesitation, Bertram decided to go to de King in de Paris ghetto leaving Helena all Billy No Mates. However, coz she was de daughta of dis well famous but dead quack doctor, she fought she could do somefing to help.

So unknown to Bertram, Helena followed him finking that she might be able to come up with de special cure for de King geeza – which amazingly she does! And all coz she was de daughta of de well famous but dead quack doctor, innit.

Well, as de King geeza is well chuffed with de bitch for saving his life, and as de sign of his respect for coming up with de cure for not being all dead, he gives her some well cool bling for her finger and tells de bitch that she could get all jiggy jiggy with one of de palace posse.

Dis was brilliant for Helena. Coz as Bertram was dere in de palace, she went all girl power and picked him ahead of all de others who was all ready, waiting and gagging for it. Bertram, on de other hand, was not. Alright, so Helena saved de King from being all stiff but even so, he

4

still fought she was de first class minger who was stalking de crap out of him, innit.

But unfortunately for Bertram, it didn't matter what he wanted coz what de King geeza said de King geeza got, which was well bad news for him. Coz as de King geeza had made de promise to Helena for saving his life, he ordered Bertram to marry de bitch and there wasn't nuffing he could do about it. He was well screwed.

Realising he had no choice he said "Aiii," and in de moment of cunning and cowardly brilliance, Bertram legged it off to Tuscany to fight in de war. So you could say that given de circumstances, Bertram preferred to make war and not lurv, innit.

Unaware that she had been shafted big time, de dim Helena returned to de Rossillion ghetto assuming that Bertram was gonna follow, but it soon became clear that her man had other ideas, de swine. Then, acting all smug and macho, he sends word to de confused little bitch saying that he wouldn't allow her to call him her sugar daddy until not only had she got his bling off his finger, but also got herself up de duff with de nippa. This, of course, was impossible coz Bertram was in de Italy turf which was too far away for them to do it togevva, which was exactly de way he wanted it.

Finally realising that he was messing with her, Helena decides to do somefing about de situation by finding out where Bertram was and following de lurv rat in de cunning disguise of de pilgrim. Eventually getting all de way to de Florence ghetto, Helena bunks in with de widow and her daughta, Diana, who, by some strange twist of fate, was de well fit babe what Bertram wanted to bone like crazy.

Well, it isn't long before Helena and Diana start yakking to each other and when they discovered what Bertram had been doing behind Helena's back, they both decided to teach de scumbag de huge lesson for doing de cruel fing by playing with all dere girlie emotions.

So without getting too bitter and twisted, Helena told Diana to go for it girlie girl and accept Bertram's offer of de big bone. However, she also told her that before they get all touchy feely with each other, Diana must get Bertram to give her his finger bling.

6

So de scene was set for Bertram to get his rocks off with Diana but when de candle was snuffed out and everywhere was filled with black, fings were about to go de shape of de pear for de two-timing sucker.

Coz as he was about to get all jiggy with her, Diana and Helena changed places and in his lurved up state, Bertram couldn't even tell which bitch was which even when they were doing it togevva. And to finally stick it to Bertram, Helena managed to swop de finger bling what de geeza King had given her for Bertram's, which was well cool of de scheming little minx.

But, perhaps, de real act of screwing with Bertram's head was de untrue rumour of Helena's death which suddenly started spreading round de hood. Everyone was yakking about it but Bertram wasn't bovvered coz he reckoned that as he never wanted de bitch anyway, and as de bitch was all dead, he was off de hook which was well cool. And coz he was so pleased that everyfing had worked out so well, Bertram legged it back to Froggyland as happy as anyfing, innit.

Sometimes, though, life has de way of getting even coz de King of France geeza recognised de bling Bertram

7

was wearing on his finger coz it was de exact same bit of bling what he gave Helena, which meant that de scumbag was well in de poo. Bertram was busted and he knew it when de King geeza arrested him on de suspicion of doing Helena in.

Dis was de crappy situation and just when Bertram fought that it couldn't get worse for him it did, when Diana and her manky widow muvva come to de palace and pointed de finger of blame at him which was not de good fing for Bertram and he knew it, especially when out of de blue Helena appeared. Not only was de bitch still breathing and wearing Bertram's bling on her finger, but she's also got his sprog in de tummy.

And so de truth was out but all was not lost coz suddenly realising de error of his ways, Bertram apologises for being de well stupid muppet and declares his undying lurv for de Helena bitch, which was well good coz everyfing was now cool in de hood.

AMLET, PRINCE OF DENMARK

Dere was somefing minging in de State of Denmark which was making Amlet all uncool. First, his Uncle Claudius had married his muvva, de main bitch Queen Gertrude. Then de Norwegian Fortinbras massive was freatening to invade de Danish turf and finally, and quite unexpectedly, de rank ghost of his nutty farva was spooking de crap out of him.

De minging ghost told Amlet he was poisoned by Claudius and wanted him to do somefing about it. Amlet said "Aiii," and reckoned de best way was to pretend to go all loony toons to make everyone fink he was barking, including Ophelia, de fit bitch he wanted to be all jiggy jiggy with.

9

Although Amlet was real good at making everyone fink that he was de first class basket case, he still couldn't believe that Claudius had killed his farva. So he came up with de cunning plan to get some actor dudes to perform de play what he wrote. A play all about how Claudius did it, as told to him by de ghost of his dead farva.

As de actors did de play, Amlet was finally convinced of what his uncle had done, and told de Queen that it was Claudius what did de murder. Unfortunately for Ophelia's farva Polonius - who had been sneakily eavesdropping behind de well huge wall tapestry – he was bricking it and panicked. Dis was unfortunate as it made Amlet fink it was Claudius who was behind de tapestry and stabbed him all dead and then stabbed him all dead again.

Now believing that de game could be up, Claudius sent Amlet off to de English turf to trick him into finking he was taking an important letter to de King of England, and got two of his posse from de hood, Rosencrantz and Guildenstern, to go with him. However, it was nuffing more than de minging trap coz what Amlet didn't know was that de letter from Claudius was asking for de King of England to make him all dead.

Meanwhile, back in Denmark, and coz Amlet had been doing his best to convince everyone he was Billy Bonkers, it was de poor bitch Ophelia who was really losing her marbles. She had gone proper nuts and had drowned herself in de river and not just coz Amlet went all pretend mad but coz her farva, Polonius, had come over all stabbed and dead behind de tapestry.

Back in England, Amlet had sussed de bogus letter from Claudius and cleverly changed it so that de execution order was for Rosencrantz and Guildenstern instead of him which meant, luckily, that he was also able to leg it back to Denmark as soon as word reached him about Ophelia.

However, Ophelia's bruvva, Laertes, steaming with de anger for what Amlet did to his family, had secretly met with Claudius and togevva they planned to mash Amlet to death.

On de day of Ophelia's funeral, Amlet yaks to his main geeza Horatio all about his well narrow escape from England. But as one death situation closes, another one opens when Laertes challenges Amlet to de duel with de pointy swords.

11

But what should have been de fight of honour is instead just de minging plot to nobble Amlet when Laertes and Claudius puts poison on de tip of his pointy sword. And just to make well sure that he snuffs it, Claudius has de poisoned cup to hand for Amlet to drink from.

And so de duel begins with de Queen Gertrude and Horatio watching, but horror of horror, de Queen mistakenly drinks from de poisoned cup and de silly bitch trips out, before dropping down all dead on de ground.

Meanwhile,. and despite Amlet getting well cut by the tip of Laertes poisoned sword, Laertes still manages to lose his grip and stabs himself with de poison tip of his own pointy sword, which was well stupid, innit.

As Laertes is dying, he is overcome with de guilt of everyfing and spills de beans about what he and Claudius really did with de pointy sword and de poisoned cup. Amlet is not happy. In fact Amlet is far from happy and makes his minging step-farva drink from de cup what poisoned de Queen, and watches him die de right horrible death.

Alas, poor Amlet, too, collapsed in de arms of Horatio, dying from de fatal sword poison, leaving de entire royal posse dead. But while dis was not really good for de Prince of Denmark and de rest of de royal family, it was well cool for Fortinbras and his Norwegian posse who were left to rule Denmark. Result.

ANT AND CLEO

Dis was de tale of two ghettos, de Roman Empire turf, run by Mark Antney, leader of de Roman hood, and de Egypt massive which was under de fumb of de well fit Cleopatra bitch. But de really cool fing about Ant and Cleo was that not only was they in charge of everyfing, but they was also boning de crap out of each other in Cleo's Egyptian yard.

But while Mark Antney was bossing it in Egypt, dere was trouble with de Pompey posse, which meant he had to return to de Rome ghetto and see Octavius, de geeza who was gonna be de next Caesar of all Rome.

Octavius was no idiot coz he knew that Mark Antney had been de naughty boy and was nobbing Cleo, and he reckoned that was well out of order. So to keep fings real, Mark Antney agreed to marry Octavius's sista Octavia, which he reckoned would make everyfing cool in de hood between him and his bro.

But fings were never de same again coz when Octavius got his promotion to Caeser, and realising that he was de marked man, Mark Antney legged it back into de arms of Cleo. When he found out, Octavius went ape with de rage and vowed to give Mark Antney de monster slap for dissing him and his sista by knocking around with de slapper from Egypt. De bruvvas were now at war with each other.

Although he had loads of army geezas advising him, Mark Antney ignored all dere expert advice to fight Caeser on de land and instead, stupidly, he listened to de Cleo bitch who told him to mash Caesar on de water.

Dis was not de smart fing to do as Mark Antney made de classic mistake of finking with his pants instead of his brains, innit. At de height of de watery battle, de stupid bitch Cleo ordered all her ships to sail away from de enemy. Then de lurvstruck Mark Antney ordered his ships to do de same fing which meant that he well screwed up.

De price of defeat soon became clear when Caesar told Cleo, out of de goodness of his heart, that although he was still gonna allow her to rule de Egypt turf, she could only do it if she wasted her scumbag boyfriend. But coz she was de sista doing it for herself, Cleo wouldn't be told and de battle continued on dry land in de muvva of all battles against Caeser.

But fings got no better for Mark Antney when Caesar once again beat de crap out of him. Dis was not de good fing and with de situation looking real bad, Mark Antney did what all geezas do in times of trouble - he blamed his bitch girlfriend for everyfing what went wrong and freatened to waste her. So with de idea of being killed not being one she cared for, Cleo told her servants to tell Mark Antney that she felt well violated and had done herself in all dead.

Oh how sad it was for him when he got de news. Coz as much as he said he wanted to slap up his bitch, now he fought Cleo had snuffed it, he felt really bad and miserable. In fact, he felt *so* bad and miserable that he fell on his own sword, fatally wounding himself with de pointy bit.

However, when he was found, and coz he was still not quite all dead, de servants took him to Cleo where they suddenly become all jiggy jiggy with each other before Mark Antney breathed his last breath and snuffed it.

Well, upon getting de news of de death of Mark Antney, Caesar suddenly began to feel sad, especially when he remembered all de wicked times they had chilling togevva in de hood. But although he was going through de grieving process, Caesar still couldn't resist sticking it to Cleo by wanting to take her as de present to himself for mashing his traitor bruvva.

But Cleo had other plans coz she didn't want to be no trophy bitch for anyone now her big boy was all dead. So she cunningly got hold of de asp snake animal, put it to her baps, and used de venomous bite to kill herself. So by coming over all dead, she proved without any doubt that de stupid bitch Cleo wasn't so stupid after all – ya get me?

AS YOU LIKES IT

Dis was de tale of two bruvvas, de Duke Frederik and de Duke Senior, who were well minging to each other and did not agree on anyfing or nuffing. They was always bringing it on with each other over fings like who was going to be de main man in de hood.

So it was only de matter of time before one of de bruvvas ran de other out of de home turf. And so it proved when de Duke Frederik got de throne and de Duke Senior didn't, and ended up bumming around in de Forest of Arden. Although he had his massive to hang out with, de Duke Senior left his well fit daughta, Rosalind, behind which didn't exactly make de situation cool or nuffing.

Meanwhile, Orlando and Oliver, two other bruvvas what didn't get on, were having issues due, in no small part, to de way Oliver was always dissing Orlando by trying to beat de crap out of him. What is it about families, eh?

Anyway, when de Duke Frederik organised de wrestling rumble, Oliver fought up de well good plan to mash Orlando by getting dis geeza Charles - de well fit champion wrestler - to rough up his bruvva by giving him de slap or even, heaven forbid, de breaking of his neck.

But miracle upon de miracle, Orlando not only sticks it to Chaz but he also gets de attention of Rosalind, which really gets up Oliver's nose. Now fings were seriously getting out of order so Orlando legs it into de Forest of Arden on account of not wanting to end up all mashed and mangled.

Anyhow, while all dis had been happening, de Duke Frederik had been up to no good by kicking Rosalind out of de home turf by telling her to pack up and do one, just like he did to her farva. However, all was not lost for de poor bitch coz when de Duke Frederik's own daughta Celia found out what happened to Rosalind, she was well miffed coz it was de well minging fing to do, innit.

De fing was that Celia and Rosalind were close bitches and just de fought of her best mate going into de exile made her feel well sad so she decided to go with her. However, and just to make fings strange but interesting, Rosalind got herself all disguised as de boy called Ganymede while Celia reckoned it would be well wicked to be Aliena, Ganymede's sista. They also took along de clown geeza called Touchstone for de company, as you do.

Orlando, though glad to be away and safe from his minging bruvva, was all lurved up about Rosalind and doing fings like writing well gooey poetry and stuff. Dis was de girlie girl he had been gagging for, and his heart was aching real bad for de sexy bitch.

Oh how strange that fickle finger of romantic fate can be coz quite by chance Orlando bumped into Rosalind, although he did not know it was Rosalind coz she was still all disguised as de Ganymede geeza – which is well confusing, innit.

But anyway, she didn't say nuffing to de poor sod as Orlando poured out his feelings to his new best friend who was really de bitch Rosalind. If only he knew.

Rosalind, though, couldn't stop herself from being in everyone's face by trying to do de bit of matchmaking for some of de forest massive like Silvius and Phebe. But Phebe didn't want to know coz she had fallen in lurv with Ganymede – who was really Rosalind, who was not a lezza. Definite.

It wasn't all bad coz at least someone was sorted when Touchstone found de bitch called Audrey to bone which, considering he was de clown, was de real result for de geeza. Sweet.

Oliver and Orlando were now being well cool with each other and decided to put dere differences behind them and be all reconciled helped, in no small way, when Orlando stopped his bruvva from becoming lion meat by rescuing Oliver from de jowls of de lion animal. Then life becomes even sweeter for Oliver when he decides to get all jiggy with Rosalind's main bitch Celia.

Meanwhile, Rosalind, still as Ganymede, was busy trying to make sure she wasn't stuck in de civil partnership with another woman by making Phebe promise to marry Silvius before telling Orlando that after having de word with Rosalind, de girl was gonna be his bitch after all. Result.

And so de parf to true lurv was finally laid when Rosalind revealed to Orlando that she was not de batty boy Ganymede but instead de well fit bitch Rosalind, which he fought was well wicked. Now everyone was cool coz they was all getting it on with each other. Phebe married Silvius and even Touchstone and Audrey decided to be man and bitch, which was well good for de clown.

But, perhaps, de best bit of all was when de Duke Senior found out that his minging bruvva Frederik went all religious and decided to be de monk, leaving his bro, de Duke Senior, to take over running de turf meaning that everyone, including de clown, lived all happy ever after. Sweet.

DE' APPY BITCHES OF WINDSOR

Sir John Falstaff was well unhappy with himself coz although he was de brave knight, he was potless and needed to get some de Niro, quick. So he came up with de cool plan to bone de couple of well minted babes, de fit bitch Ford and de even fitter bitch Page, and then get his hands on all of dere husbands' dosh.

Being really cool with de quill and ink, Falstaff wrote lurv letters to both de girlies declaring his undying passion for de bitches. But what he did not know was that de two girlie girls – who weren't into doing lezzy fings with each other - hung together in de hood and were able to compare de letters and see that they were exactly de same.

For being de rat, they decided to teach Falstaff de big lesson for being so crappy by making de minging knight look well stupid for trying to get all jiggy with them, de swine. So they sent him dere own lurv letters back saying that they couldn't wait to get his kit off, coz they were both gagging for it real bad.

So they arranged to meet up with de knight and do sexy fings togevva, but what they really had in mind was to mess with Falstaff's head. Coz while he fought he was on de promise of de lurvfest, they managed to get him to hide in de minging laundry basket, before getting it thrown into de Thames, which was well rank, innit.

Finally, though, de fit bitch Ford and de even fitter bitch Page told dere husbands everyfing what had been happening. Well, de geezas were well miffed with Falstaff for trying to mix it with dere babes and so they all decided, once and for all, to stick it to Falstaff.

However, while all dis was going on, Page's daughta, Anne, had got three geezas after her, Slenda, Doctor Caius and Fenton. Although they were all well fit, in truth, Fenton was de only one what she fought was sex on a stick, innit.

But although she was full of de hot flushes for Fenton, she didn't have time to dwell on de matters of de heart coz despite having nuffing to do with Falstaff, she was roped into de minging act of revenge and humiliation of de randy knight.

She was told to take all de children from de hood and attack Falstaff. But in order to make it de well wicked surprise, they were all cunningly disguised as fairies so as not to arouse de suspicion of de knight while he waited in de woods for de two fit bitches to come to him.

Meanwhile, in an act of fascist parental dictatorship, Page's husband pulled Slenda aside and told him to elope with Anne that very night while at de same time, de fit bitch Page pulls Doctor Caius aside and tells him de same fing too.

Coz of de fairy costumes de nippas were wearing, Slenda and de Doctor were told that Anne was gonna be wearing de well good fairy mask but even so, they would still be able to recognise her coz of de colour of her dress. And it would have been that simple but for de fact that Anne had made plans of her own, and had already eloped with Fenton. But unlike Falstaff, however, Fenton was far away from de vengeful parents.

Before long, Falstaff had been found and was well mashed by de children in de fairy costumes. It was de huge ruck and it didn't stop until de wives and husbands came forward and revealed demselves to de utterly humiliated Falstaff. And with de satisfaction of de job well done, he was lucky enough to be forgiven by de fairy posse.

While all dis was happening, Anne and Fenton secretly got married and lived all happy ever after but de same could not be said for Slenda and Doctor Caius. Slenda fought Anne was gonna be in de white dress while Doctor Caius fought she was gonna be wearing de green one. But they got so confused that they mistakenly ran off with de couple of boys instead, which was well batty, innit.

DE MIDSUMMER NIGHT'S DREAM

Lysander and Hermia were all lurved up. They were all crazy about each other but there was de small problem with dis geeza Demetrius.

Coz although he was boning Helena, Hermia used to be his main bitch and now he wanted her back which was not just wishful finking, coz that was exactly what her batty farva, Egus, wanted too.

To make his daughta do what he wanted, Egus gave Hermia de choice of what to do under Affenian law. He gave her four days to decide to choose between Demetrius, de life in de nunnery living as de penguin or getting de death sentence. De choice was easy peezy lemon squeezy for Hermia, and she legged it with Lysander into de surrounding forest.

Meanwhile, and unknown to lurv's young dream, dere was problems in de forest ghetto with Oberon and Titania, de main King geeza and de main Queen bitch of de forest fairy posse. Coz they had been arguing big time, de King Oberon decided to teach his bitch Queen Titania de huge lesson for showing no respect or nuffing. Kings don't like that sort of fing.

So de King got his servant Puck to get some magic lurv drops. De plan was for Oberon to sprinkle some on de eyes of de Queen when she was sleeping. Then, when she woke up, de idea was that she would feel all jiggy with de first fing she saw when she did de opening of de eyes.

Meanwhile, Helena and Demetrius had followed Lysander and Hermia into de forest but although they were togevva, it didn't stop Demetrius from dissing his bitch. Oberon, though, just happened to overhear Demetrius being minging to Helena and told Puck to put some of de lurve drops on de eyes of Demetrius, so that he should start treating his woman with respect, innit.

But Puck messed up big time and put de drops in Lysander's eyes instead of Demetrius. Dis was bad coz it meant that when Lysander saw Helena, he would want to bone de crap out of her instead of Hermia.

While all dis was going on, de Queen had somehow found herself with de donkey animal as her main geeza, and it was all fanks to de Puck servant messing about with de group of actors what was rehearsing de play in de forest.

For de laugh, Puck had given de Bottom actor geeza de head of de donkey. So bearing in mind what de King Oberon had done with de lurv drops to de Queen bitch, it came as no surprise that Titania had fallen in lurv with de first fing she saw when she woke up – even if it was de actor with de donkey's head called Bottom.

However, when Oberon found out that Puck had made de pig's ear of trying to get Demetrius and Helena togevva, de main King geeza took matters into his own hands by personally getting de bit of de lurv potion onto Demetrius, making sure that Helena was de first bitch he saw. But instead of being grateful, de poor bitch was well miffed coz she fought that both Demetrius and Lysander were having de laugh, innit.

At dis point, Oberon decided that enough was enough and he put all of them into de deep sleep. Then, and just to make sure that nobody else was confused, de King geeza gave Lysander de antidote for de lurv potion so that he would lurv Hermia when they all woke up. Then, finally, Oberon gave his own bitch, Titania, de antidote so they was able to be all jiggy with each other once again.

When Lysander, Hermia, Helena, and Demetrius awoke, they were all well confused but fought it was nuffing more than de really bad trip – which was well wicked, know what I'm sayin'?

DE TAMING OF DE BITCH

Baptista, de weathy merchant geeza of Padua, had two daughtas, Kafferina and Bianca. But instead of being happy, dis family had issues and all coz of Kafferina. Dis sista had no respect for nobody in de home turf which everyone fought was well minging of de bitch. She was de ghetto Princess with de really mean attitude but could she be told? Of course not coz you couldn't tell that bitch nuffing.

It got so bad that her farva finally had enough of de ungrateful bitch dissing everyone in de turf, and decided that nobody in de hood was gonna marry de younga daughta Bianca until Kafferina had learned some respect and settled down.

As far as punishments go it was well out of order coz de only one who was really suffering was Bianca - and it wasn't even her fault! Worse still, dere was dis geeza Lucentio from de Pisa turf who wanted to get it on with Bianca. All he wanted was for her to be his bitch but coz of Kafferina's well bad attitude in de hood, no way was it gonna to happen. Or was it?

Lucentio decided that he wasn't gonna give up on Bianca but realised that in order to get close enough for him to get it on real heavy with de bitch, then he had to come up with de clever plan, which he did. He decided that he would swap places with his servant Tranio and by switching freads and being all disguised and that, Lucentio would then offer his services as de tutor for Bianca in order to get de bitch in de mood for de big bone.

Meanwhile, and unknown to Lucentio, de geeza from de Verona massive called Petruchio, was coming to de Padua ghetto to chill with his main man Hortensio who, by some strange coincidence, also wanted to be all jiggy jiggy with Bianca. Man, she was one hot bitch! But de real surprise to everyone was that Petruchio actually found de stroppy Kafferina de real sexy turn-on.

In no time, Baptista, de batty and de much relieved farva, agreed for Petruchio and Kafferina to marry. However, realising that she was still de stuck-up minger, Patruchio set out to tame de bitch and would wind her up by saying fings like "Know yourself little girl," and "Am I bovvered," to whatever she said, which was well cool.

Eventually he wore de mouthy bitch down until Kafferina was all tamed and chilled. But not only that, de bitches little sista Bianca finally got it on with Lucentio, which was well wicked. Even de geeza Hortensio got lucky after losing out on Bianca, and settled for de well minted widow in de Padua yard.

At Bianca and Lucentio's wedding rave, Petruchio starts larging it with his posse and makes and wins de bet that he had de most obedient bitch of all de bruvvas in de hood. But de best bit of all was when Kafferina gave Bianca de lecture on how to be de heavy and lusting bitch herself, to which her little sis said "Aiii."

JOOLS CAESAR

Jools Caesar was de man with de plan in de Roman massive, who was getting maximum respect for mashing de minging Gauls and de Pompey warriors. Even his bro Mark Antney fought he was de main man, but not everyone was so cool with Jools. De senators, for instance, didn't like de way he'd been larging it and was being so wicked with everyone. They weren't happy with him bossing de turf like he owned it and they was desperate to do somefing about it.

Although they really wanted to stick it to Jools more than anyfing, de senators knew that dis was not gonna be easy. However, de senator geeza Cassius had de cunning plan when he decided to have de quiet word with Brutus, who was de bruvva who knew Jools best from everyone in Caeser's posse.

Dis was de really cool bit of finking coz Cassius knew that Brutus was not stupid or nuffing and could see that wasting Caeser would be brilliant for everyone in de Roman yard. And he was right coz Brutus said "Bring it on, coz I is well up for it, man."

Meanwhile, Jools's bitch Calphurina had de women's intuition and told him to watch out for de posse of men who wanted to give him de good kicking. Even his soothsayer said that he should beware of de minging ides of March, so he couldn't say he wasn't warned or nuffing but still Jools was being too cool for his own good and took no notice.

Dis was not good coz de next time he was hanging with de senate massive it was to prove real bad for him. Coz de moment his back was turned, it was all stabbed with de pointy swords by Brutus, Cassius and de rest of de disloyal senate scum, innit.

So with Jools all dead, Mark Antney was not happy with what de senators did to his bro, and came up with de plan to get even by getting Brutus to allow him to speak at Jools's funeral. And dis was de cunning masterstroke of all masterstrokes.

Mark Antney gave it his all with de "Friends, Romans and de Countrymen" speech, as he worked de crowd up by dropping everyone who killed his mate Jools deep in de poo-poo. What began as somefing sad but chilled, ended with everyone in de crowd calling for de blood of Cassius, Brutus, and any other minger associated with de death of Jools Caesar.

Now de gloves were off and as de assassins began to cack demselves, Mark Antney got togevva with Jools's nephew Octavius and his massive to beat de crap out of all de traitorous scum in de hood. And they was well ruthless as they went after as many of de enemies as they could, including de armies of Brutus and Cassius.

As everyone fought against each other, and knowing that he couldn't win, Cassius fell on his own pointy sword. Brutus, too, made himself all dead rather than be taken captive, leaving Mark Antney to take charge of de Roman turf and to hang with de rest of his posse, which was well cool.

MACBEFF

Macbeff and Banquo were two bruvvas from de hood and part of de well wicked King Duncan massive. They hung togevva and were always getting maximum respect from all de boyz in de ghetto.

All was well in de home turf until one day after they mashed de Thane of Cawdor, they encountered three rank witches who gave them de heavy prophecy. De three mingers hailed Macbeff as Thane of Glamis, de next Thane of Cawdor, and de future main King geeza. So you could say that as far as prophecies went, it was well wicked for Macbeff.

Banquo was also like de cat animal who got de cream after he was hailed as de daddy of all de future kings which although wasn't as cool as Macbeff's prophecy was still, nevertheless, cool enough for him to feel well wicked with himself. So with de prophecies all sorted, de three rank witches sort of evaporated into nuffing leaving Macbeff and Banquo finking that they'd just been on de muvva of all trips, man.

Nuffing more is said until King Duncan tells Macbeff that he's gonna be de next Thane of Cawdor as de reward for being de well top geeza. But behind every top geeza is de pushy bitch and when de Lady Macbeff finds out about de promotion, she starts to fink that as cool as it was to be for her geeza to be de Thane of Cawdor, it was nowhere near as cool as being de main King geeza – even if it meant getting Duncan wasted.

Macbeff wasn't crazy about whacking de King but his bitch just kept nagging and nagging and nagging with all her, "Yeah but no but yeah but no," stuff, until finally she got her way to put her evil plan into action. And knowing when King Duncan was going to be in de castle turf she planned to get his massive all drunk, which would then allow for Macbeff to get to de King, cut his froat with de pointy dagger, and plant de evil instrument of bloody death on de King's drunken posse. Sorted.

And so it happened, but Macbeff felt like de right old minger for what he did and started to feel all tripped out when he kept seeing de blood-soaked dagger floating in de air, which sort of spooked de crap out of him.

It was fair to say that Macbeff was not in de good way and de same went for his scheming bitch too. But, nevertheless, Lady M still managed to muster up de inner strength to return to de scene of de crime to plant de dagger on de posse after Macbeff wouldn't. But still de fat lady did not sing.

Coz when Duncan's body was found, Macbeff flipped and went all Texas Chainsaw by whacking all de posse with de pointy sword. Maybe it wasn't all his fault coz rage and grief affects everyone differently but even so, is mass murder really an excuse?

Anyway, now crapping demselves, Duncan's sons, Malcolm and Donalbain, both leg it in case they were going to be next which was wicked for de Macbeff's. Coz with nuffing now standing in his way, Macbeff was crowned de main King geeza of Scotland, just like de minging witches had said.

However, Banquo was not convinced all was exactly kosher, and also remembering de witches, he was dead suspicious of what had happened. Call it de well heavy guilty conscience and that, but Macbeff knew Banquo was looking at him all funny which made his bottom go well sweaty with de fear of being found out. So as preparations for de celebratory coronation banquet rave were being made, Macbeff put out de contract to get rid of Banquo and his son Fleance, which was de well minging fing to do.

Although Fleance got away, Banquo was all done in which should have made Macbeff feel well good. But that night he was visited by de bloody ghost of Banquo who said he was so not happy. Macbeff said he wasn't bovvered but you know what, he bloody well was.

Meanwhile, his bro Macduff had also done de bunk to de English turf coz he reckoned that Macbeff was bang out of order. Well, when he found out, Macbeff went ape with de rage and butchered everyone in Macduff's entire household. It was now crystal that fings had got way out of hand and that was why Macduff decided to join forces with his main geeza Malcolm in de England turf, raise an army, and get Macbeff sorted.

As he waited for Malcolm and Macduff to try and beat de crap out of him, Macbeff was given another prophecy by de witches who said Macbeff wasn't gonna be all dead by de hand of any geeza born of de bitch. So while he was beginning to feel pretty cool, de same couldn't be said for Lady M who, on de other hand, was losing it big time before killing herself all dead.

As de English armies were approaching, most of Macbeff's massive were legging it as far away as they could. Dis was not exactly de really good time for Macbeff to find out who his mates were. Bummer. And so de battle began with everyone larging it with de other, but Macbeff was still de man coz nobody could take him down. Nobody, that was, until Macduff.

But what of all de "born of de bitch who can do him in all dead" stuff, as told by de minging witches? Well, although Macbeff fought he was all sorted he was, in fact, up de creek without de paddle. In other words, Macduff was delivered by Caesarian section which, technically, was not de same as de natural birth and born of de bitch and therefore, in de nutshell, was screwed, innit.

From then on there was de really good news and de not so good news. De not so good news is that Macbeff fights a bit with his pointy sword but ends up getting his head all chopped off, which Macduff keeps as a souvenir. However, de really good news is that Malcom is crowned King of all Scotland which is well good.

MEASURE FOR DE MEASURE

incentio, de Duke of de Vienna turf, decided to take time off from being de Duke and chill, so he made his main man Angelo his deputy to rule in his place, which Angelo fought was well wicked. But all was not what it seemed.

De actual reason de Duke decided to take de break was that he was real crap at handling all de rank behaviour of fings like happy slapping by de hoodies in de yard, and so he gave Angelo de permission to do somefing about it before de home turf became de no-go ghetto.

It was no surprise that Angelo took to being de pretend Duke like de duck to de orange sauce, coz he was de evil sadistic scumbag. However, what de psycho stand-in Duke did not know was that de crafty real Duke had put him in charge of de hood, knowing that if anyone was gonna be unpopular for taking care of de home turf, then it was not gonna be him. But instead of going off, as Angelo fought, de real Duke secretly remained in de hood disguised as de holy friar geeza in order to keep an eye on fings.

But all was not cool in de yard. Angelo's enthusiasm in carrying out his duties took everyone in de ghetto by surprise, especially dis geeza called Claudio, when he was arrested for getting his bitch Jules up de duff before they was hitched. Dis was not good for de young couple as de sentence for de crime of getting de leg over and getting bitches pregnant with de sprog was death, innit.

Dis was well minging and so Claudio's well fit sista, Isabella, legged it over to Angelo and begged for her bruvva's life. Now, coz Isabella was an untouched girlie girl and was about to become de well holy nun, she reckoned Angelo would change his mind and let Claudio off with an ASBO or somefing. But unlike the busted Claudio, de psycho replacement Duke was having none of it.

However, not being one to ever give up she just kept on and on until, eventually, Isabella's pleading and beauty finally got de result – although not de sort of result she was planning on exactly. Sure, Angelo agreed to free her bruvva, but he made it crystal that it was only gonna happen if he got his end away with de virgin Isabella by not making her de virgin no more.

Shocked by de fought of being treated like de turf slapper, Isabella turned de nasty substitute Duke down and legged it over like de clappers to de prison and told her bruvva all about it. However, instead of being all shocked and outraged, Isabella was left feeling well miffed when Claudio understandably said that he was more than happy to swap his sista's virginity for his life. Selfish, yes. Stupid, no.

Meanwhile, and unbeknown to de concerned little bitch, Vincentio, de proper Duke, and still in his clever friar disguise, just happened to be around and secretly listened in on de conversation. It was at that moment he finally decided it was time to do somefing to save both Claudio and Isabella from dere dire predicament. Lucky for them, de Duke had de well good cunning plan.

He knew of de pretty little bitch called Mariana, who was once engaged to Angelo, and was still gagging for him real bad. So acting quickly, and still dressed as de holy friar geeza, he managed to persuade Isabella to pretend to accept Angelo's offer except for when de moment came to actually *do* it with de pretend Duke.

It was then and only then that Mariana and Isabella would swap places with each other. So with everyfing planned to de last detail de last fing anyone expected was for de plan to go de shape of de pear but it did, and all coz Angelo decided to execute Claudio anyway, de swine.

Coz he was still all dressed up as de friar geeza, when de Duke got de minging news he didn't panic or nuffing like that. De first thing he did was to persuade de jailer to switch another condemned geeza for Claudio and execute him instead. Dis was well good for Claudio but de real bummer for de other geeza who was still gonna be all dead anyway.

Next he then told Isabella that she had been well and truly stitched up by Angelo but it was all gonna be alright coz he wasn't just de innocent kind-hearted friar geeza.

Oh no, he was in fact de real Duke in de friar's disguise. And without another word he grabbed both de bitches and headed off to de Vienna turf to finally sort out Angelo.

When Isabella and Mariana came face to face with Angelo and made dere accusations, he was well bricking it. In desperation he said that de bitches were lying mingers and he hadn't done nuffing, before making it worse for himself by blaming de pretend friar for everyfing. However, when Vincentio revealed himself as de friar, Angelo couldn't do nuffing but frow himself on de mercy of de Duke.

Thankfully Claudio was still alive and Mariana, de caring but misguided bitch, pleaded for Angelo's life. And with that, de Duke ordered Angelo to marry Mariana and for Claudio get it togevva with his Jules. As for de Duke, well, he and Isabella got all jiggy jiggy with each other and decided de bitch would become his lady Duke.

MUCH ADO ABOUT SOD ALL

After mashing his bruvva Don John and his massive, Don Pedro, de Prince of de Arragon turf, decided to chill with Leonata, de governor of de Messina ghetto. Everyfing was well cool in Leonata's yard that even de couple of Don Pedro's posse, Benedik and Claudio, was larging it with some of de bitches in de hood.

Unlike Claudio, who was getting all sloppy with Leonato's daughta, Hero, de parf of true lurv was not so smooth for Benedik, who was getting loads of grief from de governor's niece, Beatrice, with all her nagging and stuff. But while Benedik and Beatrice carried on giving each over de verbals, de relationship between Claudio and Hero had not gone unnoticed by Don Pedro.

Never one to miss de opportunity for de course of true lurv to run all smooth, he arranged with Leonata for them to get hitched. Now feeling well pleased with himself, Don Pedro tried to make Benedik and Beatrice fall in lurv with each other too.

But he realised that to make Benedik and Beatrice all jiggy jiggy with each other, he would have to be cunning by not only enlisting de help of Leonato and Claudio, but also Hero to send de secret messages of lurv to make Benedick and Beatrice fink that they were both gagging for it.

Meanwhile, with de marriage of Claudio and Hero getting ever closer, Don John had started to hang once again with his bruvva Don Pedro. But what nobody knew was that he really fought Claudio was de minger and was secretly planning to wreck everyfing with de bit of mischief making, like yakking to Claudio that Don Pedro wanted Hero as his own bitch.

And so he came up with de rank plan of bringing Hero's virtue into question. He did dis by getting de different bitch to be de pretend Hero and then got her togevva with Borachio, de bro from de hood, to pretend to be giving Hero de big bone. Dis was de well minging fing to do to de sad little bitch, but dere was nuffing she could do about it. She was stuffed well and good.

Sadly for Hero, de plan was successful and Claudio dumped her right at de altar in front of everyone, de swine. Now not knowing what to do next, her farva hid her away, with Leonata telling everyone that his daughta had died of de shame and of de grief of finking that everyone fought she was de turf slapper.

And Don John would have got away with it too if it had not been for his pesky bro Borachio getting wasted after de night out on de booze, boasting how well minted he was for helping de evil Don John with his rank scheme.

In no time at all Borachio was busted, and coz he was nuffing but de huge coward, he confessed to everyfing which, despite everyone in de hood finking she was all dead, restored Hero's reputation. Unsurprisingly, Leonato was well miffed with Claudio and wanted to give him de massive slap for being de first class git with no respect or nuffing, and he demanded de public apology for being so minging to his daughta.

But despite dis, and coz he was de well decent geeza, Leonato told Claudio that he was still gonna allow him to marry one of his nieces. But what Claudio didn't know was that one of de nieces was in fact none other than Hero herself.

Dis was brilliant coz Claudio and Hero was all reunited which made de entire ghetto posse well pleased that de bitch was not all dead, innit. And coz everyone in de hood was so happy, Benedik and Beatrice also decided to get all boned up togevva, which was well cool.

And so they all had de wicked rave which was made even better when they got word that Don John had been busted. Sorted.

OFFELLO

De beautiful turf of Venice was not looking so beautiful for Iago. In fact, it was looking well crappy coz he found out that de lieutenant promotion he had been hoping for from Offello, had gone to some other geeza called Cassio instead.

Feeling well dissed, Iago fought that dis was well out of order and so he decided to take his wicked revenge against de both of them. De only question was how. Then it came to him when he remembered that Offello had secretly married de fit bitch Desdemona, and so he decided to use her to get his own back.

It wasn't long before de opportunity came when Offello was sent to de Cyprus ghetto by de Duke of Venice, and togevva with his own bitch Emilia, Iago escorted

Desdemona dere to meet up with Offello. But it was only when they eventually arrived in Cyprus that Iago put his most devious and cunning plan into action.

First, he tricked Cassio into getting well mashed with de booze and then he got him into de heavy ruck with some geeza called Roderigo. De cause of de fight was Roderigo's old flame Desdemona, who Iago had said was still gagging for him. Perhaps it would've been different if he had known she was all married now to Offello, but Roderigo never asked and Iago never said.

De plan worked and Cassio was busted and given de heavy demotion which meant that Iago could continue to make trouble – and he did. Meanwhile, and still pretending to be his bro, Iago told Cassio to go to Desdemona and ask de bitch to beg with Offello to get him de rank of lieutenant.

And so Iago pushed on with his evil plan of revenge as he managed to get Offello to where Desdemona and Cassio were yakking togevva. As Offello watched de two of them rapping with each other, Iago put it into Offello's head that Desdemona and Cassio are all lurved up with de big bone.

Offello didn't know what to fink but matters were made worse still after Iago managed to get hold of de hanky what belonged to de Desdemona bitch, and plant it in Cassio's room. He then told Offello that he saw Cassio with his bitch's snot-rag.

But as bad as that was, de evil revenge plot was about to get even worse when Offello asked Desdemona about de hanky she said it was lost, which was true, but it only got lost as far as Iago, who was up to further mischief by giving de hanky to Cassio.

Coz knowing that Offello would be eavesdropping, Iago had de conversation with Cassio about de geeza who now had de hanky. However, de way it was coming across to Offello, it looked like it was Cassio who was banging on and on about Desdemona.

Now smouldering with de rage, Offello lost it big time and told Iago to waste Cassio, before turning his accusing finger at Desdemona. In front of Iago's bitch wife Emilia, she pleaded her innocence that she didn't do nuffing wrong with Cassio. But because of Hankygate, Offello was not listening and throttled de poor bitch to death, which was well sad.

While dis was going on, Iago had sent Roderigo to whack Cassio but he messed up big time. So Iago did Roderigo in so that he couldn't be grassed to Offello. But all was not well coz when Emilia discovered what happened she went all mental, not believing that Iago, her loving geeza husband, could do de murderous and minging fing.

But slowly she put it all togevva and worked out that he was indeed de criminal mastermind for everyfing that had happened. But when Iago couldn't stop Emilia from trying to bust him to Offello, he stabbed her with de pointy blade and legged it but, fortunately, he was still busted.

As for Offello, well, forced with de shame of having done in his innocent and most beautiful bitch, he stabs himself with de pointy blade and dies next to Desdemona on de bed by her side. What a waste, innit.

RICHARD DE FIRD

Richard's got issues. Although he was already de Duke of Gloucester, he was not happy coz what he wanted more than anyfing was to be de King of all England.

However, dere was already two reasons why de King fing had not happened for Richard which was his older bruvvas. De first bruvva, Edward, was already de King and de second bruvva, George, de Duke of Clarence, who was next in line to de throne if anyfing unfortunate happened to Edward's young nippas.

So de first fing he did was to get George busted after falsely accusing him of treason, but he knew that it wasn't gonna be so easy to nobble de other bruvva. But then Richard had de stroke of good luck coz while he had arranged for George to be whacked in prison, Edward, who had been really ill, snuffed it. Result.

But before Richard could celebrate, dere was de snag of Edward's nippas and particularly Eddy Jr, who was de next in line to be de King. Dis was not good for Richard coz that meant that he could only be de substitute King until junior was all grown up and old enough to be crowned de proper King of England.

So, Richard had to come up with de cunning plan to make de palace massive fink that he really liked his nephews and didn't want them all dead or nuffing. And in de stroke of real evil genius, he got everyone in de turf to believe that coz he was de caring Uncle geeza, and for dere own protection to make really sure that nothing unfortunate could happen, he arranged for his nephews to be put into de Tower Of London.

But not everyone was convinced by dis act of care in de community, and Richard knew it and that was why he arrested everyone who might want to protect de young

Princes and got them all executed so that they couldn't protect de Princes no more.

Next he got his rank bro Buckingham to tell everyone in de hood that both of his dead bruvva's nippas were real proper bastards, de swine, which meant that they weren't allowed to be King anyway. Them were de rules which meant that, surprise surprise, de parf was clear for Richard to be crowned de King of England. All of it, innit.

But still not everyone was happy with what Richard had done, including his own muvva, coz let's face it nobody knew de bloodfirsty minger like de bitch what gave birth to him. But his muvva aside, and realising that more had to be done if he was gonna be King, Richard got one of his posse to waste de little Princes in de Tower of London. How unfortunate.

But despite murdering his nephews, it didn't mean that Richard didn't like his family and that was why he wanted to bone de crap out of his niece, Anne, who was de daughta of his dead bruvva, King Edward. However, Edward's widow, Elizabeth, had other plans for her daughta coz unknown to Richard she had secretly agreed that Anne would marry de Earl of Richmond geeza.

De fing was that Richmond was not de big fan of Richard and that was why he was bringing his posse over from de French turf to mash him. Before long, de armies would come face to face in de battle of Bosworth Field. But while Richmond was psyching himself up, Richard was visited by de rank ghosts of all de geezas what he had killed, who told him he was gonna lose big time.

At de ruck at Boswell, Richard was knocked off his horse animal and cried out "De horse animal, de horse animal, my kingdom for de horse animal." But before he found de nag, Richmond was dere before him, ready to do battle with de pointy swords. It wasn't long before he had killed de evil Richard and got himself crowned as 'Enry de seventh, King of all England.

And not only was dis how de Tudor kings began dere reign but it was also de end of de War of de Roses – de battle that is and and not de chocolate, innit.

ROMEO AND HIS FIT BITCH JOOLS

Verona was de turf of de feuding Montagues and de Capulet families. And coz they was always brawling and stuff, de Prince of Verona told them to cool it or else they was gonna get well mashed if they carried on larging it with each other.

Meanwhile, whilst all dis was going on, Romeo, from de Montague posse, had become all jiggy jiggy with de Rosaline bitch who was de niece of de Capulet massive.

But never ready to settle with just de one bitch, Romeo and his boyz disguised demselves and crashed de Capulet turf where dere was de masked ball going down, and that was when he saw de well fit Capulet's daughta, Jools.

Romeo was immediately struck by her beauty and immediately realised what it was he had to do. Impressing her with his freads and bling, he pledged his lurv to Jools who was standing above on de balcony overlooking de garden. Later that night, with de help of Friar Laurence, they got married in secret.

And they would have lived all happy ever after if it had not been for Jool's cousin Tybalt, who discovered that Romeo had crashed de ball, and decided to challenge de Montague scumbag to de duel with de pointy swords.

But seeing how Romeo had secretly married his bitch Jools, he wasn't too keen on de ruck, so he sent his main man Mercutio to take up Tybalt's challenge. All went well until de big M died in de duel, which really miffed Romeo. In fact, he was so miffed that he decided to avenge his mate's death and kill Tybalt himself.

Now dis was not de good fing as de Prince of Verona got wind of all de blood and de gory goings on, and he banished Romeo from de Verona turf. Meanwhile, and coz her family did not know de bitch had married de member of de Montague filth, they tried to palm Jools off onto Paris, her crappy cousin.

So once again relying on Friar Laurence, they devised de cunning plan to stop de poor bitch from cacking herself. He got her de herbal remedy which was meant to leave her well wasted and pretend dead for forty-two hours, which would give Friar Laurence enough time to get de word out to Romeo so that he could rescue her.

Oh but fate can be so cruel coz de letter from Friar Laurence was delayed and Romeo heard from somebody second-hand that his bitch Jools was all stiff. Now full of de grief and de heartache, Romeo knew that life wasn't worth all de bling and freads in de hood, and faced with living without his fit bitch, he scored some poison and tried to get to Jools's pretend tomb to die at her side.

Meanwhile, and unbeknown to Romeo, Friar Laurence had discovered that de plan had gone de shape of de pear, and was legging it like de clappers to take Jools away until he could set fings right. But unfortunately, for all concerned, events were about to get well worse. By de time he got to de tomb, Romeo encountered Paris who was also feeling quite miserable as he fought he was gonna marry de bitch Jools.

Romeo, though, was not in de mood for sharing his grief and slayed Paris with his pointy sword before entering de tomb, finding de pretend dead Jools, and drinking de poison.

Well, when Friar Laurence entered, finking that fings could get no worse, Jools woke up coz she wasn't really dead at all. And then she saw Romeo who was. Bummer. Now inconsolable with de grief, de sad little bitch took de dagger from Romeo's belt and plunged it into her heart, this time making her really dead and not just pretend.

Arriving too late, togevva with de Prince of Verona, de Montague and de Capulet posse demanded to know what had happened, leaving Friar Laurence to tell of de tragic tale of Romeo and Jools's secret marriage and senseless suicides. It was only then, when faced with such sadness, that de Montagues and de Capulets vowed to put an end to all dere bitching forever.

And they all lived in peace and harmony except for Romeo and his bitch Jools, who was both well dead.

TWO GEEZAS OF VERONA

wo bros, Proteus and Valentine, made dere way from de Verona turf to de Milan ghetto. And while Valentine was well up for de trip, Proteus was all miserable coz he was missing his bitch Julia.

Valentine, though, was missing nobody coz he was feeling real good like he knew he should and all coz he was going to be part of de Duke of Milan's massive, which was well cool. But what was even cooler was falling in lurv with de Duke's beautiful daughta, Silvia, even though she was Thurio's bitch. However, despite Thurio being well minted and having more freads and bling, Silvia decided that she was gonna dump him and elope with Valentine.

But of course de parf of true lurv for Valentine was never gonna be easy, especially when his so called bro wanted to bone de same bitch as him. So when Valentine confided in Proteus what he and Silvia was about to do, Proteus told de Duke geeza all about it, which was real minging.

Feeling well dissed, de Duke banished Valentine from de Milan turf and slung de ungrateful bitch Silvia in de jail while making Proteus his new best bruvva in de hood. And as time passed, other fings had been happening with Valentine. Coz ever since he was busted, he started to chill with de band of evil outlaws and was made de leader, which was well wicked.

Meanwhile, back in de Verona yard, Proteus's bitch, Julia, all fed up of hanging by herself, had come to Milan looking for him. Although she was well fit with de great baps, strangely she had come all dressed up as de pageboy, as you do.

But how strange fings happen coz as luck would have it, and still in de pageboy disguise, Julia ended up working as de page to Proteus. But although she was weeing herself with all de excitement of being reunited with her man, she said nuffing when he didn't recognise her. As disappointing as it was, dis was also just as well coz what she didn't know was that Proteus had been trying to get all boned up with Silvia.

Silvia, though, was getting well miffed by all dis unwanted sexual harassment and was doing her best to have nuffing to do with de minging lurv rat Proteus. In any case, what she was gagging for was Valentine and she was gagging for him real bad. This bitch was on heat, man.

Dere was only so much she could stand and when it got to de point where she could take no more, Silvia finally did somefing about de situation and amazingly, miracles of all de miracles, somehow escaped de prison in search of him.

Well, as soon as de Duke geeza finds out about Silvia legging it, he goes after her togevva with Thurio, Proteus and Julia, de pretend pageboy. Obviously dis is not what Silvia wants but as fate would have it she was captured by Valentine's posse as she tries to get away from de Milan ghetto.

But before Valentine can get it togevva with de lurv struck bitch, Proteus catches up and snatches Silvia away and declares *his* undying lurv for her. Realising that maybe it was better to make it up instead of falling out with his bro, Valentine decides to wimp out and leave them to it.

At dis point, it all becomes too much for Julia who, when seeing her man larging it with Silvia, drops down to de ground in shock. Mind you, as it turns out, dis shock was not as big as de one Proteus got when he found out that his pageboy was, in fact, his Julie.

And now with everyfing out in de open, Proteus realises what an unfaithful minger he was and gets it back on with Julia, leaving Valentine and Silvia to get it on with each other. Sweet.

Printed in the United Kingdom
by Lightning Source UK Ltd.
132036UK00001B/4-195/P